001272766

HDQ

1 COMPACT

DISC

DATE DUE		
5/24/00	JAN 0 3 2013	
JUN 20 '00	JUN 24 2013	
JUL 18 '00	OCT 05 2013	
MAR 10 '01		
OCT 19 '01		
DEC 22 '01		
MAR 13 '02		
ILL 7-29-02		
AUG 20 '03		

5/00

JACKSON COUNTY
Library Services

HEADQUARTERS
413 West Main Street
Medford, Oregon 97501

HDQ

David Bennett
COHEN

TEACHES
Blues Piano

VOL. 2

A Hands-on Course in
Traditional Blues Piano
Featuring a Comprehensive
Audio Lesson on CD

Dedicated to Devin Nelson Bischoff

Cover Photo by David Burton

Audio Editor: George James

Mastered by: Ted Orr

Recorded at
Nevessa Productions, Woodstock, N.Y.

ISBN 0-7935-8857-X

EXCLUSIVELY DISTRIBUTED BY

7777 W. BLUEMOUND RD. P.O. BOX 13819 MILWAUKEE, WI 53213

www.halleonard.com

Visit Homespun Tapes on the internet at
http://www.homespuntapes.com

PIANO *Listen & Learn*
HOMESPUN MUSIC INSTRUCTION

David Bennett
COHEN
TEACHES
Blues Piano
VOL. 2

Table of Contents

Introduction

Blues is a form of folk music, and as such is usually not played the same way each time. The solos that I have included in this lesson, although written, are only meant as a starting point. Once you learn them, think about changing them. Don't be concerned with improvising the entire verse, but with changing one phrase, or even one note, at a time. Also, try incorporating the various riffs or musical phrases that I teach into your improvisations. The idea is to try and build a large "bag of tricks" that you can dip into whenever you play.

Your goal should be to develop your own style. Please don't be so concerned with copying someone else's solo exactly. It's the differences and the "mistakes that work" that will help you to develop your own unique style.

Please listen to as many piano players as you can. Some whom I recommend are Professor Longhair, Otis Spann, Memphis Slim, Tuts Washington, all of the Pinetops (Smith, Perkins, etc.), Johnnie Johnson, Allen Toussaint, Dr. John, Barry Goldberg (if you can find some of his recordings with Michael Bloomfield or Steve Miller), Mark Naftalin (from the Paul Butterfield Blues Band), Corky Siegal, Huey "Piano" Smith, Fats Domino, Jerry Lee Lewis... and the list goes on.

I highly recommend "The Real Honky Tonk Piano" by Tim Alexander; "Gospel Piano," by Ethel Caffie-Austin; and Dr. John's various instructional tapes, videos and CDs, all from Homespun Tapes.

I know that I've said this before, but I feel that it bears repeating: Always try to listen to what you are playing. Exercise and develop your taste. If it sounds good, keep it. If you are playing something wrong, then unlearning it is learning something new. It doesn't matter whether you are playing at home or at a gig, every time you play you are practicing because it makes it easier for the next time you play.

So, the best advice I can give is to keep playing.

David Bennett Cohen

◆ Intro Music

Medium Boogie

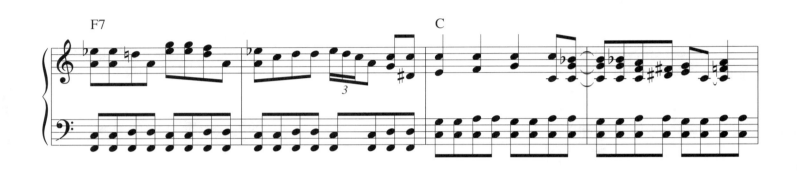

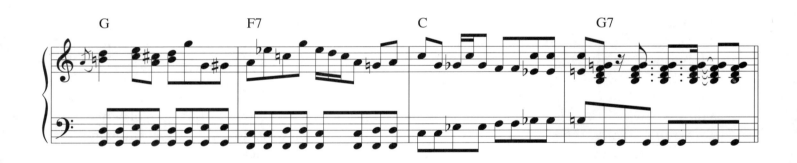

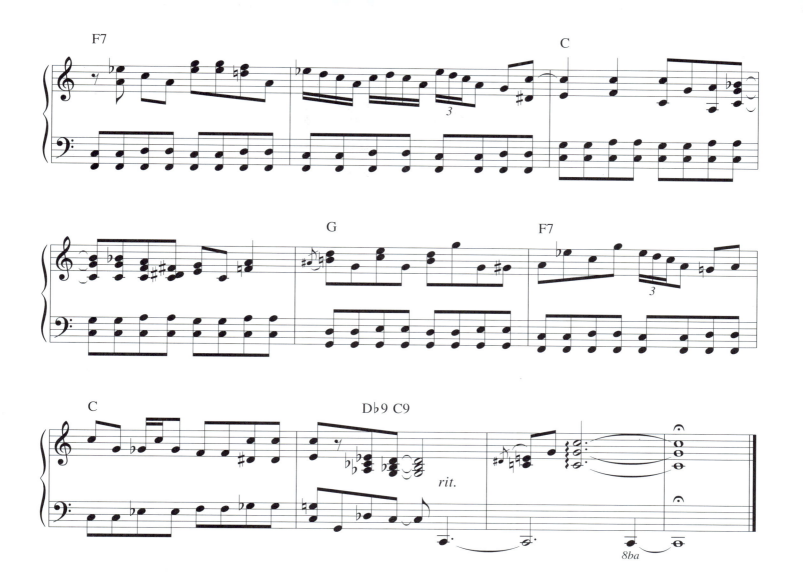

Straight Time Eighth Note Rhythm

❸ Shuffle and Eighth Note Rhythm Compared

Example 1 - Shuffle Rhythm

Example 2 - Eighth Note Rhythm

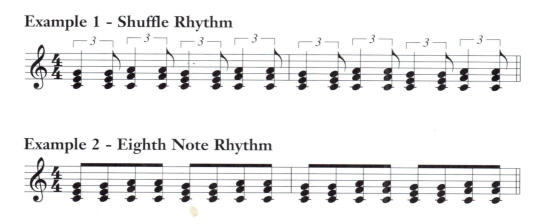

⑤ Eighth Note Rhythm

⑦ 1st Alternate (12-Bar Example)

10 2nd Alternate

12 3rd Alternate

14 4th Alternate

16 5th Alternate

17 6th Alternate

18 7th Alternate

20 8th Alternate

22 Mixing the Alternates

26 9th Chord Eighth Note Rhythm Example

28 Solo Number 1 with Eighth Note Rhythm

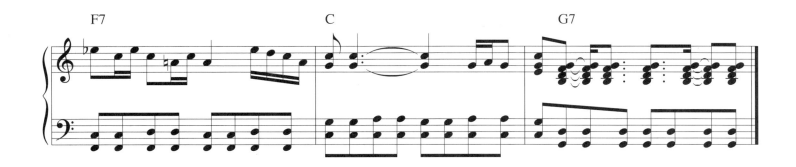

◆29 Solo Number 2

◆31 Solo Number 3

Insert at measure 10

33 Improvising with the Blues Scale

Basslines

Walking Bassline Example

37 Walking Bassline with Solo Number 1

38 Walking Bassline with Slow Blues

39 "Fats Domino" Bassline Breakdown

40 "Fats Domino" Bassline with Soloing - Example 1

Example 2 - with Minor Blues Scale

42 ◆ Quick IV Chord - Example

43 ◆ Boogie Woogie Bassline

8ba throughout

44 ◆ Boogie Woogie Bassline - Example

8ba throughout

◆45 Boogie Woogie Bassline - Breakdown

8ba throughout

Boogie Woogie Bassline with Solo - Example

8ba throughout

49 Bass Coming Out

8ba throughout

51 **Straight Time Boogie - Example**

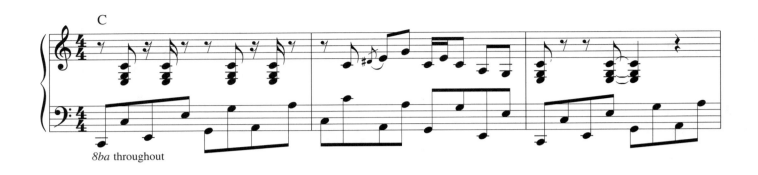

8ba throughout

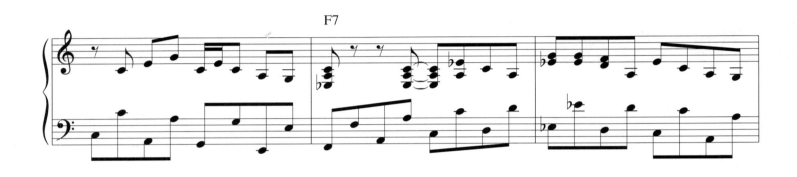

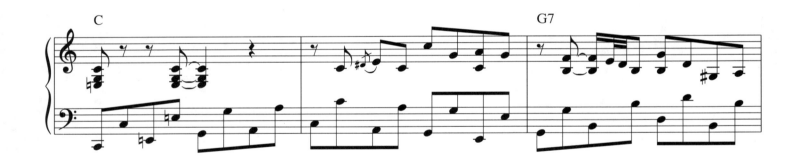

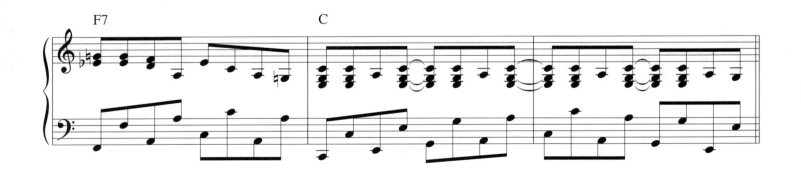

Higher Example

New Orleans Rumba Bassline Number 1

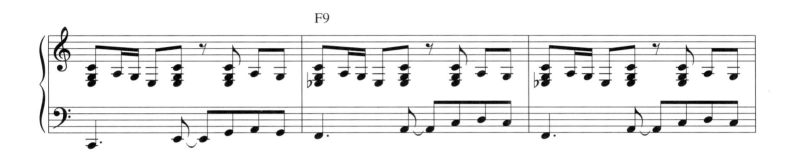

56 Rumba Number 1 Breakdown

⬥57 Rumba Number 2 Breakdown and Example

+ 8ba throughout

58 ◆ Rumba Number 2 with Solo

◆59 Walking Up from C to G Chord

Insert at Bar Eight of 12 Bar blues

+ 8ba

Turnarounds

◆60 Turnaround - Talk

Example 1

Example 2

◆61 1st Turnaround - Chromatic

◆62 2nd Turnaround - Tenths

◆63 3rd Turnaround – Thirds

64 4th Turnaround

65 5th Turnaround

66 6th Turnaround

67 7th Turnaround

68 8th Turnaround

69 9th Turnaround

70 10th Turnaround

71 11th Turnaround

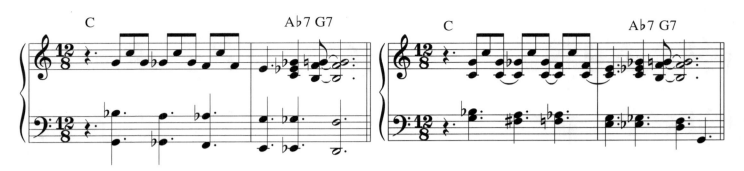

72 12th Turnaround

73 13th Turnaround

Endings

74 ## Example 1

75 ## Example 2

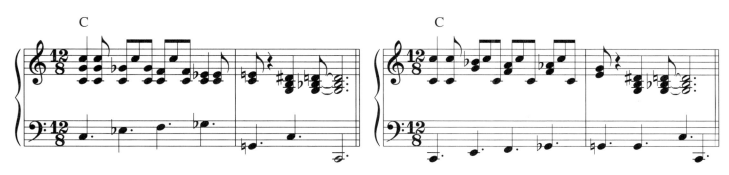

76 ## 1st Ending – with Stop in Bar 10

🔷78 2nd Ending

🔷79 3rd Ending

🔷80 4th Ending

◆81 5th Ending

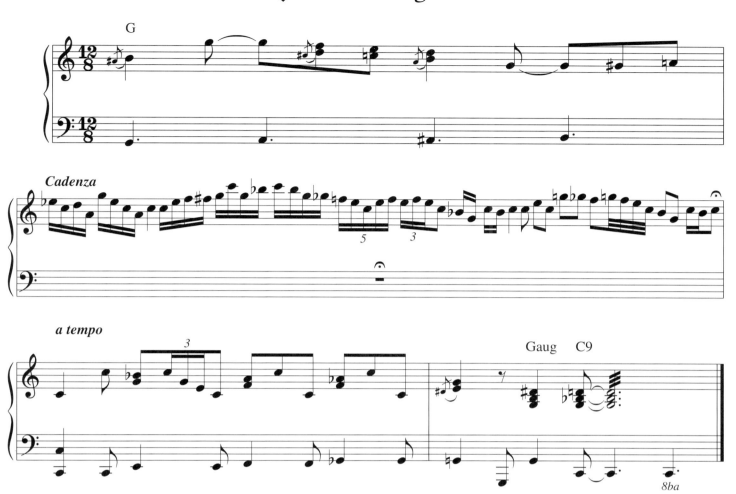

◆82 6th Ending

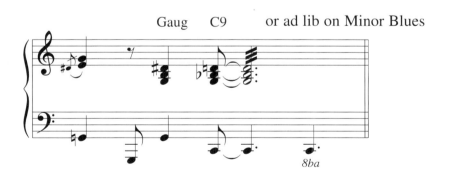

◆83 7th Ending - White Key Gliss

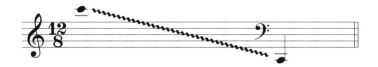

◆85 Outro Music

mf

8ba throughout

HOMESPUN®
LISTEN & LEARN SERIES

This exciting new series features lessons from the top pros with in-depth CD instruction and thorough accompanying book.

GUITAR

Russ Barenberg Teaches Twenty Bluegrass Guitar Solos
00695220 Book/CD Pack................................$19.95

Rory Block Teaches Classics of Country Blues Guitar
00699065 Book/CD Pack................................$19.95

Cathy Fink and Marcy Marxer's Kids' Guitar Songbook
00695258 Book/CD Pack................................$14.95

The Guitar of Jorma Kaukonen
00695184 Book/CD Pack................................$19.95

Tony Rice Teaches Bluegrass Guitar
00695045 Book/CD Pack................................$19.95

Artie Traum Teaches Essential Chords & Progressions for Acoustic Guitar
00695259 Book/CD Pack................................$14.95

Artie Traum Teaches 101 Plus Essential Riffs for Acoustic Guitar
00695260 Book/CD Pack................................$14.95

Happy Traum Teaches Blues Guitar
00841082 Book/CD Pack................................$19.95

Richard Thompson Teaches Traditional Guitar Instrumentals
00841083 Book/CD Pack................................$19.95

BANJO

Tony Trischka Teaches 20 Easy Banjo Solos
00699056 Book/CD Pack................................$19.95

PIANO

David Bennett Cohen Teaches Blues Piano
00841084 Volume 1 Book/CD Pack..................$19.95
00290498 Volume 2 Book/CD Pack..................$19.95

Warren Bernhardt Teaches Jazz Piano
Volume 1 – A Hands-On Course in Improvisation and Technique
00699062 Volume 1 Book/CD Pack................$19.95

Volume 2 – Creating Harmony and Building Solos
00699084 Volume 2 Book/CD Pack................$19.95

Dr. John Teaches New Orleans Piano
Volume 1 – In-Depth Sessions with a Master Musician
00699090 Book/CD Pack..............................$19.95

Volume 2 – Building a Blues Repertoire
00699093 Book/CD Pack..............................$19.95

Volume 3 – Sanctifying the Blues
00699094 Book/CD Pack..............................$19.95

HARMONICA

Paul Butterfield Teaches Blues Harmonica
00699089 Book/CD Pack................................$19.95

John Sebastian Teaches Blues Harmonica
00841074 Book/CD Pack................................$19.95

PENNYWHISTLE

Cathal McConnell Teaches Irish Pennywhistle
00841081 Book/CD Pack................................$19.95

FOR MORE INFORMATION, SEE YOUR LOCAL MUSIC DEALER, OR WRITE TO:

HAL•LEONARD®
CORPORATION
7777 W. BLUEMOUND RD. P.O. BOX 13819 MILWAUKEE, WI 53213

0198